Acknowledgement and Dedication

Eye of the Beholder would only be words spoken if I didn't hold the drive, vision, and will to divulge intimate pieces of my life through poetry; it is these personal experiences in life, including the good, the bad, the beautiful, and the ugly that I invite readers to observe and behold. I want to thank every person I've ever met because pieces of you inspired every word in this book. I would also like to thank my family and friends for all their support and for always believing in me. This book is a testimony of overcoming obstacles and enduring passion, ambition, and a will to live. I would like to dedicate Eye of the Beholder to everyone that has been a part my life. I would also like to thank Jacob Frank (front cover photograph), Marie (book cover and back cover photograph), Dr. Christine Keaney and Amanda Rodriguez (editors) for their assistance in helping produce Eye of the Beholder.

I0086945

www.adrieldavis.com

Table of Contents

The One At the Beginning

6/4/79 was the day my dad said you'll be mine
They decided to bump and grind
And on 2/21/80 a one of a kind was born
Maybe he was out his mind
But he saw something in momma eyes
That no one could deny
Defied the odds
Labeled as odd
Too big to fit in
When the wind blows
He weathered the storm
So from 2/21/80
He was determined to make it
So thanks to 6/4/79
Cause the world is mine
And I will always be
One of a kind

The One About Moving On

Moving back
You are such a sweet talker
Sweeter than sugar
You had me at hello
All I wanted to say is goodbye
Carrying your seed
You could care less
I was the best for you at the time
You want to bump and grind
With anything moving
Well I am moving-on
I'll love you forever
But I must forge on
Your son is born
I refuse to raise him
As a child of the corn
Moving on

The One About Leaving

Gone forever
You'll never see me again
We committed a sin
Sex before marriage
I was so young
And yet I wasn't dumb
You let your cum
Enter my eggs
Now we are moving ahead
Well you left in the past
I am packing my bags
Going away
You can stay
I have your seed
I refuse to let him grow amongst the weeds
You'll never see me again
We committed a sin
But my son is not a sin
He will win
Sit back and see
Gone forever

The One Against the Odds

Born a little too soon
And already against the odds
I can't see
There's no oxygen going to my brain
Will I live or will I die
I can't make my momma cry
When she barely knows who I am
We been together for almost seven months
And now fate wants to dump trouble in our path
She prayed and God rescued me
Born a little too soon
No need to worry
I can see
Mom, you can finally introduce me to the room
Nearly blind, and entering the world a little too soon

The One About a Hard Beginning

One day at a time
I know it's just me and you
I refuse to be more pain
I've seen what you've been through
These little eyes have seen so much
When you give me that mother's touch
I know it's pure love and joy
At times you couldn't buy my toys
But you always provided for me
So when I get older
You'll see
I will make you proud
Watch me transform
From a boy to a man
It may be earlier than planned
But I was destined to be Momma's little man

The One In the Morning

Not today
That is just a dream
At two years old
Under the cabinet
On to stovetop
I was ready to eat
Each and every day
But hey, it's time to wake granny
As I do every day
She said honey I'm tired
Not today
I love you, granny
I wanted your food each and every day

The One About Me and You

Just me and you
Mom we on our own
What are we to do
You working all these jobs
Just to provide for me
I ain't old enough
But thanks to you I can see
The joy in your heart
The pain in your eyes
The wear on your body
The faith in your soul
Me and you together
Makes everything whole
Just me and you

The One About My Sister

I will never know who you are
I never got a chance to meet you
You were taken away from me, before I could see
What you and I would be
Little sister, I know God had a plan
But in 1983, I was just too young to understand
One thing I promise you
I will grow up to be a great man
I am just sorry, I never got a chance to touch your hand
You would have been my sister
I would have been your big brother
I am sorry mother that you had to carry the pain
Of not meeting your daughter in 1983
God has a plan; just wait and see

The One At Age 7

It's so sad
I was such a pain
I wanted to play games
Putting my mom to shame
Always in trouble
Frequent visits to the principle's office
I felt I was my boss
Lost in my own action
It's so sad
I am only seven
And I have my mom going mad
I was such a pain

The One About School Blues

Summer School
Man, I don't like
I was way too smart
But my actions told a different tale
I should have had my tail beat
For the things I was doing
Ruining my future
Before I even had one
Sent to summer school
To clean up my act
Acting a fool
I was too smart
I just didn't use it in school
Summer School Blues

The One On Stage

I had to prove a point
At such an early age
I was in rage
Always on stage for my friends
I had to prove a point
My teacher said I wouldn't pass
That my behavior would come and bite me in my ass
I wasn't going back to second grade
That wasn't cool
I wasn't about to be no one fool
So I tighten up
Cleaned up my act
That was the day I decided to finally get on track
I had to prove a point

The One About Hard Times

Mother
Times are hard
And I can hear your cry
I can't lie; I want to cry with you
But what can I do
I am not old enough to work
So how do I help ease your pain
When I am not old enough to even
Change my diaper
I still need your help, but I want to help you
So what do I do
This mind is already light years ahead
I can see and feel more than most
Just give me a chance
And one day you'll
Cruise the coast
Mother
Times are hard
And I can hear your cry
I can't lie; I want to cry

The One About Stolen Joy

With my very eyes
I seen what happened
No eight-year-old should see this type of pain
What did I do to have this done to you
You were only four-years-old
And your body was cold
I couldn't hold on
Because you were like my brother
Because you raised by my mother
We were like peas in a pod
Oh God, why did this happen to me
I had to sit in the back of the funeral
Because this pain couldn't be real
I am only eight
And life is already stealing my joy
I am only eight, and I feel I can't take any more
With my very eyes
I seen you go cold

The One About Moving

It was time to go
I didn't want to go
Momma said we moving
But what about my friends
She said if I keep you here
You'll grow up in a life of sin
I know you don't understand
But trust in me and you will see
It's time for change
And change you will see
I am removing this image
You have created in your mind
Cause burying you
It's one thing I refused to do
So give me all your clothes
I am throwing them away
Because there is a new you
And he is here to stay
We moving
And you're moving on from
This image in your head
Cause my son
Will not end up dead
It was time to go
So get that street life out your head

The One About a New Place

This new place
Mom, I love our new house
And I have a sister on the way
This has become my happiest day
We are no longer in the hood
You moved us to the woods
But this would be the place
That laced my well-being
Seeing myself grow
With a healthy environment all around me
I see what you did
Thank you
I am a very blessed kid
I love our new place

The One About Losing at 11

March 3rd, 1991
God came and took your hand
Man, did he get a great man
The stories, the knowledge, and the lessons
I couldn't ask for a better man
You were a blessing
Served your country
Even fought in the war
You opened the door
For so many
And you blessed me plenty
I was only eleven
March 3rd
You gave your last words
And went to serve a better place
I just pray
I see you another day
March 3rd, 1991
The day they took you away

The One About Granddad

You preached to me
Because you were a Preacher
You reached me at an age
To keep me away from the streets
I would meet amazing people
Because of the values you instilled
It's so surreal that you are still embedded in all I do
You didn't preach at me
You preached to reach my soul
To hold on to these words
So you can spread your word
So many years later
And Granddad still lives on
I know I was so shocked
When the world took you away
But I know it was time for you
To go to a better place
I just wish I was nine
When I lost you
I almost lost my mind
Granddad, I love you
I just wish we had more time

The One About Ms. Allen

Ms. Allen was a dream
She saved my life
I was physically alive
But mentally dead
I had lost grandfather
It was all downhill
She helped me apply the brakes
She seen my decline
She was a gift
That kept me from losing my mind
Ms. Allen was dream
She was one of a kind
She saved my life

The One About Ms. Coleman

Dear Ms. Coleman
You were such a star
You seen something special
Before I even knew it myself
Pushing me to be better
Not settling for anything less
You wouldn't accept anything but my best
I was prepared to cruise
Because school was so easy
But you laid down the law
And wanted me to shoot for the moon
You seen a star in your eyes
You just needed me to open my eyes
You seen something special

The One About Friends with Guns

I was only ten
I had these friends
They were my boys
They weren't playing with toys
They had guns
Replacing books in the bag
For a gun in hand
Man, why did my mans
Have to go and do that
Now they are expelled
It felt like hell
I was only ten
And they are toting guns
I just wanted to have fun

The One About Lessons Learned

Why would you call me a nigger
Just cause my skin isn't the same
You are only ten
And already playing the racists' game
Who taught you such a bile way of life
You called me a nigger
And I took matters into my own hands
Man, and I paid the cost
Sent to the principle
And almost sent away
What a day
What a lesson learned
He called me a nigger
And I was the one who got burned
At ten year's old
What a lesson learned

The One About the Southside of Town

Southside of town
You treated me right
You gave me sight
Planted a seed
To make my future bright
Southside of town
Where the Falcons soar
You opened the door
For that I can't ask for more
Southside of town

The One About Butterflies

I was so shy
I can't lie
You approached me
And I had no words
I wish I could tell you
How you gave me butterflies
How just a glimpse
Could bring light to my day
I just wish I knew what to say
On that day
You approached me
And I couldn't even say
Hey
I was so shy
I can't lie

The One About the Street

You taught me the streets
So I could survive
You told me
To stay out
Cause no one gets out alive
You told me boy you way too smart
For your own good
So find a legal way to get your mother out the hood
I would teach you more
But I don't want you to get too deep
I need to have peace when I sleep
Knowing you are doing fine
You way too young
To know these ways
Listen to me
Stay away from these streets
I wish had done the same
Now me and my brother
Have expired from the game
And the only one to blame
Is ourselves
Sorry our act was short
I know you were only eleven
But rest easy
We found our way to Heaven

The One About the Fire

Up in flames
What happened that day
I can't say
We came home
And it was no longer a home
The fire had clearly
Torn down our dome
There is no house; there is no home
Up in flames
Along with the memories
Thanks to mom
She rebuilt the house
Made it a home
Up in flames
But still a home

The One About Long Walks

Long walks to you
Because you couldn't walk the same
I felt your pain
When they took it away
You lost a part of you
And I lost a part of me
I could see things had changed
You were just as beautiful
Despite the change
Long walks to you
Kept me sane
You were my Granny
All of my heart
Long walks to you
Cause you touched my soul
Long walks to you
Rain, Heat or Storm
Granny lost a limb
But I am the one who mourned

The One About the J's

Olympic J's
I seen you from a mile away
I yearned for the day
I could have you on my feet
I couldn't sleep
Thinking of our union
I worked all summer
Day and Night
I had you in my sight
Olympic J's
We were miles away
I searched night and day
I couldn't find you anywhere
Then you appeared
And it was no longer a dream
I used all my summer money
To have you near
Then granny came
And said take this money
It's not funny
My dear
You worked all summer
Used all your money
That was a bummer
All for those Olympic J's

The One About Growing Up

Growing up way too fast
I wanted to last
But I was running
At the speed of light
I was fighting with myself
Fighting with life
I wasn't sure if I could survive
So many broken pieces
And stuck putting myself back together
Whether I am coming or going
I felt like I was fading away
Growing up way too fast
I felt I would be gone
Because I could even have my first piece of ass
I was growing up way too fast

The One About June 22, 1992

June 22, 1992
What do I do
I no longer have you
I never been a man that cried
But I couldn't stop on that day
Why would they take you away
You were embedded in every fiber of my being
Now I am seeing you in a casket
As if life hadn't already torched me enough
It stole from me the woman I loved the most
You were the glue that held generations together
You managed to have a big enough umbrella
When everyone was facing stormy weather
June 22, 1992
I'll never know what to do
I lost my heart
Because my heart was you
So in honor of you
I will one day tattoo
Psalms 27
Over my heart
So I can always be close to you
June 22, 1992

The One About the Village

Ripped and torn
I could only mourn
You were more than my heart
You were my very being
I couldn't see a day without you
What do I do
I can't keep taking these losses
I am falling to pieces
Because a piece of me is leaving with every loss
I am running out of time, and I can't keep paying the cost
Please let me go; I can no longer bare
Without you being around
Grandma, I called you Ma
You were my village
You were my heart
I can't keep going
You had my heart
You spoke to me after you were gone
You said I know you can't speak of your pain
So take what you feel
And put that pen and paper to work
It will heal your pain
It will solve your problems
You may be ripped and torn
But always remember
Life goes on

The One About the DUI

DUI
You crushed our car like it was a can
Man I had my whole family in the car
Why can't I stand
You changed my life
And all that it would be
We ended up in a ditch
While they let you slip past the system
Privileged and protected
For reasons unknown
DUI
While me and my family were on our way home

The One About Saving Grace

Saving grace
It was her peaceful sound
Although she wasn't around
Her spirit spoke to me
Always carrying me when I fell
Always giving me a second wind
When I had run out of breath
She was my heart
And no longer in physical form
She had conformed to my heart
And my very being was seeing
Life as she wanted it to be for me
I may no longer see you here
But I know you're there
I love you
I still feel you here
Even though you're there
My saving grace

The One About A Breakaway

Man what a time
I was with family
Cuz and I out playing some ball
When I had a breakaway
And up up, and boom
There should have been a call
Knocked out
As if the lights on the street were gone
When I came to
My only question was
"What did Jordan do?"
I was in a daze
Hand in cast
From three fractures
Man what a time
I wish it wasn't mine
That had to be broken
But later in life
That was an experience
And now it is spoken

The One About Footsteps

Footsteps tracing my past
Telling a story
That I wish could disappear
History haunting me like
Ghosts of Christmas past
Footsteps behind me
Following closely on my ass
Trying to make it to the shoreline
So they will no longer see
The traces of my footsteps
That I hope will no longer be
Footsteps tracing my past

The One About Christmas Day

On Christmas Day
I thought Santa had passed me up
Shook and shocked
Because there wasn't anything under the tree
Mom could see the tears in my eyes
I was good all year
I had gotten good grades
I traded all my bad habits
To become a young man
I just couldn't understand
Why there wasn't anything under the tree
Then I went to Granny's
And the joy that would be
Then saved the day
All I can say
Her and mom wouldn't have any other way
On that Christmas Day

The One About Winning

Never quit
I gave you a will to win
You will be faced with troubles
Again and again
Be strong
Lead with your heart
And you will never go wrong
Never quit
I gave you a will to win
You'll be faced with troubles
This world is full of sin
Never quit
And you'll always win

The One About Pain

Something ain't right
I can't move like I want
I know this pain ain't real
I been to all these doctors
All they saying
Is he growin' still
I know my mind; I know my body
So something ain't right
Why when I jump
I can no longer take flight
Momma, something ain't right

The One About the Game

There is no spot for me
I tried out
And I got cut
I had the skills
I didn't understand the game
It was a shame
I had all this game
With all these skills
I was overthinking
Sinking deeper and deeper
There was no spot for me
I had to see the bigger picture
And see the game was for me
It just took time for me to see

The One Where I Fight

Out of the dark and into the light
All my life I've had to fight
For the right to be right
Trying to erase my sins
Writing with this pen
To cover up these acts
I repeat and react
Because I've always been under attack
Out the dark and into the light
All my life I've had to fight

The One About High School

Welcome to high school
The game has changed
I am getting into my own
Finally learning the meaning of my name
Welcome to high school
Time to shed being a boy
And start turning into a man
Welcome to high school
The game has changed
It's time to finally know your name

The One About Studying

When will it end
I was just a freshman
And the load was so heavy
Late night studying
Until my brain wanted to explode
What a load for a boy so young
This isn't any fun
I want to run
But this was a gift
IB was such a trip
When will it end
I was sinking fast
I just wanted to know how long would this last

The One About Surgery

Why are they cutting me up
Like I am a piece of beef
I am only fourteen
And they said my knee is shot
How can they take my hops
When life hasn't even given me a shot
Are my dreams shot
Is this the end
Mom, why does he have a knife
Is this where my life starts or where it ends
Why are they cutting me up

The One About Rehab

Rehab
As if I was in a lab
Trying to rebuild the man I used to be
Crying in so much pain
Rehab
Got me going insane
I am too young for this to be real
Doctor, if you don't get right
You'll never be right
So I had to get in the right mind
So I could put all this pain behind
Focus on my career
Before darkness comes
And decided to steer
Rehab
I hate you
But I love you dear

The One About Being Dropped

I was asked to come to top
Then I got dropped on my head
Feeling like I just got marked by the Feds
How could you rob me right in front of my eyes
Telling me lies
Recruited to play varsity
Politics dropped me to the Freshman team
What do you mean
My dreams will come true
Now I am blue
Questioning myself on what to do
I guess it wasn't my time
But I'll never forget
This scenario will play as a loop
I was dropped and I didn't know what to do

The One About Support

Support me
As I learn to grow
Show me the way
For that's something I do not know
Support me
I am ready to grow
I am a sponge
Ready to soak up the knowledge
Support me
As I learn to grow

The One About the Journey

Things aren't perfect
But they never will
We must take this journey
No matter how it feels
Things aren't perfect
But they never will
Fill your heart with joy so it can feel
Steal a moment of joy
To soothe your soul
Things aren't perfect
And they never will
Just stay on the journey
And enjoy how it feels

The One About Granddad

Lightning strikes again
And I felt it in my bones
For some reason I knew you weren't coming home
Then they came to my class
And for some reason I knew
This wouldn't be the last time
I would feel this way
Another day
Another loss
I had lost another loved one
Granddad you were the best
I don't know why
But I knew something was wrong
When I felt that pain in my chest
Lighting had struck again
And I had been hit
And it hurt quite a bit

The One About Choosing

I had to realize my worth
Scared to have a voice
Just always taking it on the chin
But how can you win
When all you doing is taking the beating
Battered and bruised
People cruising over your feelings
I had to realize my worth
Scared to have a voice
I had to make a better choice
And the choice had to be me

The One About Games

You played me
And that was cool
I was younger
But I was no fool
You stood me up
Under the worst way
I would lie and say I'll never forget that day
But you weren't worth it
You laughed and giggled
And thought it was a joke
But looking back
I have no regrets
You did me a favor
That I am willing to bet
You played yourself
Not me
I was just too young to see

The One About My Friend

Man she was so fine
She had the whole school
Drooling over her
Chasing her like a quick high
She wasn't trying to be no cheap thrill
She knew the real in her heart
She had caught my eye
I can't lie
But she was just my friend
Man she was so fine
I had to get those thoughts out my mind
She had the whole school
Drooling over her

The One About Being Robbed

Man what joyous time
Some new j's had dropped
And I had the scoop
I was heading to cop the new j's
Cash in hand
But the clock was running thin
We had to hit the road
Pockets full of cash
Road trip to prove our skills
We killed their dreams
But the joke was on us
Robbed behind our backs
I had to travel back home
In the same gear from the game
Took my money for my J's
But we took the game
A short lived joyous time

The One About Wrong Place, Wrong Time

Wrong place, wrong time
Man, I must be out my mind
Sitting on the set
Chilling with friends from school
Then a group of fools
With some random beef
Want to come with some heat
People scatter, you can hear their feet
Wrong place, wrong time
Man, I must be out my mind
Sitting on the set
Almost got caught up
And have my life ended
With a slug to the chest
At the end I was blessed
I won't speak on the rest

The One About the First Time

My first time with you
I know it felt right
Yet, it was something we shouldn't do
You were older
But I was so mature
What can I say
You opened my eyes
My first time with you

The One About Late Nights

Late nights with the crew
We had connects
So we knew what to do
Hanging out chilling
Running like we were wild
Thinking that we grown
When we were really just a child
Late nights with the crew
I am thankful
That I made it out those times
Without being in the system
Or catching a case
Because they wanted to put us away
Just because of our race

The One About Becoming a Man

Momma, I am ready to work
She said no
I said how will I ever know
If you don't ever let go
I know what I need to do
Thanks for the wisdom
I have a vision
And it's very clear
Just give me a chance
I love you, momma dear
I need to start growing on my own
Before I am forty and still at home
Let me go get this job
So I can become my own man
I am fine
You can let go my hand

The One About Brothers and Uncles

I got your back
We were brothers
Even though you were my uncle
You taught me what I needed to know
Looked out, since I had no older brother
You smothered me in knowledge
Until my brain would overflow
How did I know
That the things you taught me
Were things in life
I needed to know
Huggie Bear
I know you care
Thanks for always being there

The One About Being Stopped

Officers it wasn't me
What I can't see
Is why we being stopped
We got all our stuff in line
Why are we being
Pushed around
We are a "suspect"
What do you suspect us of
Hours later
Like we the patronages and you're the server
Serving us some lies
Cause you was misinformed
And didn't recognize
You were looking for someone of another skin
And I am sure this will happen again
Officer it wasn't me
I am sure I will say those words
Over and over again

The One About Friends

Internet pen pal
You were more than a gal
Speaking as if we were neighbors
But we were miles apart
We started to build
Even though we couldn't chill
Then we both graduated
End up in the same school
Oh man, that was so cool
The tables had turned
We were kind of lost
We were young
But full of promise
Until you had to leave
I couldn't believe it was gone like that
And years later
Thanks to social media
We jump right back
Internet pen pal again
Just like that

The One About the Final Stretch

The final stretch
This is the last year
Dear God, what a journey
Filled with twists and returns
I've learned so much
Yet, we have so far to go
I know, I am in your hands
I know it's time for me to become a man
The final stretch
This is my senior year
I know I should have so much to fear
But it's my calling
It's time to rise
There is no way I am falling
As I hit that final stretch

The One About Stars

I was a star
You were a star
Man did we both shine
I know on paper I could call you mine
But in my mind, you weren't mine
We drew so much attention
Did I mention
That you were special
But, I think we were too young
Too young kids
With chips on our shoulder
Later in life, I'll see you again
We just need to get a little older

The One About Numbers

I wish this would pass
Why do they keep robbing my ass
I am tired of getting jacked for my cash
Taken from behind my back
Man, can they cut me some slack
While we out here putting up numbers
They steady robbing us, taking our numbers
From gear to jewels to even cash
They have to have an inside plug
They keep robbing our ass

The One About the Senior Trip

I missed the bus
I don't even cuss
But I missed the damn bus
Spooked, Shocked, and Torn
I was mourning
I had to regroup
They were gone
So I felt trapped
Got on the phone
And me and mom rapped
She schooled my dad
She said this is all he had
Fresh on a plane
Back in the game
Made my Senior trip
Man that was insane
A time I'll never forget
Mom and Dad delivered
When I thought my senior trip was dead

The One About Getting Out

It's time to decide
And I don't know where to ride
Should I stay home
Or roam
I just need to find a fit
But mom said get your shit
Cause you need to leave
You need to become a man
If you don't leave Tallahassee
You'll end up in a body bag
She said staying here isn't an option
So let's find you a place
If you don't get out of here
Boy, you going to make me catch a case
It's time to decide

The One About UF

Off we go
I don't want to be here
She said there is nothing to fear
I said it's not about the fear
I don't like this place
It's not my taste
She said, do you trust in the Lord
And do you trust in me
I said yes
She said then you will see
So give it some time
You'll see what I mean
You're going to UF
That's where you should be
Trust in the Lord
He knows best
You'll fail a lot of tests
But you'll come out better
And you'll rise above the rest
Just go to UF

The One About Leaving the Nest

Time to leave the nest
You have been given the tools
To be the best
You are no longer under their wings
But you still have God's angels
Looking over you
So go and do what you got to do
Remain true
To who you were raised to be
And you'll look back
And you will see
That leaving the nest
Was the best thing to do

The One About Preview

Preview of my world
While I was at Preview
The stars were aligned
And fate was set
I met UF's most important connect
Filled with dreams and desires
To make a change
How would I know
I would be forever in her debt
The week of preview
Thank God
He already had my life set

The One About My Crew

They became my crew
We were just scrolling
Trying to learn what to do
We started talking
And boom
One of the homies said come through
We walked for miles
Like strangers in the woods
What could this be
We all wanted to see
But that day
Friends for ever
And at the time no one could see
How close random friends
Could one day be

The One About Faith

Mom I am ready to go
This ain't for me
She said open your eyes
So you can see
God has put forth a plan
And there is nothing you can do
Just accept his word
And let him do what he do
You're young, and truly can't understand
But trust in God, as he turns you into a man
But mom I am ready to go
Listen to me son
Put your faith in God
And never run
Open your eyes
So you can see

The One About Lovers and Friends

You started as my friend
Time and Time again
We spent every waking moment
Until we got to the end
So many precious moments
So many words
Just no communication
We heard words
Just didn't understand the meaning
Friends to lover
We were like no other
We spoke to one another
Just hide behind a cover
We got to the end
And found nothing but problems
Lying under the covers
We started as friends
Ended as past lovers

The One About First Love

To my first love
I know you questioned
What we were
And, I know it made you feel lost
I didn't know love
So I paid the ultimate cost
Growing up, I only knew
The love of a mother, father and of family and close friends
And in the end
I was told being in love
Made you soft, even told it made you weak
But I fell asleep
Caught in the most pleasant dream
Full of happiness, joy, and peace
The only catch is this wasn't a dream
It was love
And I didn't recognize it
Twenty-four hours ripped us a part
I wish I had rummaged through the wreckage
To find what we lost
But we both let it slip
I lost my first love
All because of one power trip

The One About Love

What is love
I really didn't know
I had a good one
But somehow let her go
I pray that from this day forward
I will learn what love is
So I can fix this pain
So I can regain
Some of the pieces of me
That I lost
For not knowing
What love is

The One About Grief

When things fell apart
I made you carry the grief
I made you feel like it was all your fault
I taught myself to push the pain on you
I hate that I wouldn't allow you to be free
I gave you all the burden and all the pain
Now you carrying baggage that belongs to me
Even though you're miles away
And time has passed
I haven't gotten past the things of the past
They haunt my very being
All these skeletons are re-appearing
And I am fearing they are here to stay
Just grant me one day
To erase this grief
When things fall apart
I made you carry the grief

The One About Walking Away

Walking away
Oh what is the pain
I have decided it's time to leave the game
So many years dedicated
So many sacrificed seconds, minutes, hours, days and years
So many tears
So many fears
I love you to the core of my heart
But I need to restart
My body is battered and bruised
I know this comes as shocking news
I am walking away
Hanging up my shoes
I am leaving it all on the court
Time to transport my talent
To a book, since I left the other part of me
Splatted all over the court

The One About Forever

This can't be real
How did you steal my heart
Was it because you seen the broken pieces
And helped put it back together
Or did you see me as a rebound
And decided to endure the stormy weather
This can't be real
Feels out of this world
In my heart
I think
I've found my forever girl
This can't be real

The One With No Hope

All time high
And I don't even get high
So many amazing years
Until she decided to get high
Tearing down all we had built
Lacing her joints with lies
Lying next to me
And me feeling the person change
Racking my brain on a way to save us both
But in the end there was no hope
I lost the love of my life to dope
While on an all-time high

The One About Promises

Here is my promise to you
Never overdo your love for another
Never settle for less than you deserve
You've poured out your heart and soul
Only to be left in the cold
Mold yourself into the man you want to be
Let the world see
What you are destined to be
Here is my promise to you
Remain true to who you are
Never let anyone drive your car of life
Be the leader of your future
Leave your past in the past
And if they don't understand you
Simply let them kiss your ass
Here is my promise to you
Past self to present self to future self

The One About Her

She caught my eye and she didn't even try
I can't lie
There was something about her
She had it
But I made the wrong call
She still had baggage
And refused to throw it away
If she had
Then that day would be our day
I consoled her, warmed her
But she was too blind to see
She was hanging on to a past
And couldn't see me
She caught my eye and she didn't even try
She was special that I can't lie

The One About New Beginnings

New beginnings
Man what a hard ending
I have moved away
From the place I knew all too well
I had to bail
Because it was becoming a hell
I was free, but felt like I was in jail
New beginnings
Tragic endings
That is part of life, losing and winning
To my new start
I am happy
You have captured my heart

The One About Us

We met by accident or maybe it was fate
Someone gave me the key
I opened up the gate
Only to find you
And I didn't know what to do
It had been awhile, but man did I like you
I travelled miles to see you
Just for us to study
We acted like a couple
But on paper were buddies
I seen your potential
And wanted to see you glow
But you hit me with a left blow
And took all we had
And let it go
I wish I stayed silent
Instead of caring so much about
Seeing you grow
If I had
Maybe you would have never let us go

The One About Being Tired

Tired of running
Tired of these games
Roller coaster rides
Bumper car city
Stuck in a place full of silicone bitties
I ain't talking about your titties
Talking about you
I can deal with the silicone titties
I can't deal with the silicone you
Tired of running
Tired of these games
Surrounded by silicone people
Who only want to play games

The One When Things Fall Apart

When I knew
I didn't act
Now I am packing my bags
Since my heart has left
I had it all within reach
Yet, I wouldn't grasp her soul
She wanted to stay
But, knew she had to leave
All she wanted was my heart on her sleeve
She sent me messages
Made all the calls
I didn't answer
So it all fell apart
Her love, the heart she had for me
She told me I held a special place in her heart forever
She loved me and would miss this sunny weather
But she needed to leave
Cause she couldn't love me again
No matter the weather, or whether it would destroy me or not

The One About You

On days that I am lost
I find myself thinking of you
It was like being on a constant high
But you're the drug
And no adverse side effects
On days I am lost
I would pay any cost
Just to have you within my reach
This was a lesson; I wish life didn't have to teach me
I can handle being lost
I couldn't handle losing you
So when I am lost
I am lost until I find you again

The One About Moments of Joy

You've meant more to me
Than I could ever imagine
When I think of moments of joy
They all included you
Parts of me are blue
Knowing I'll never have you
Parts of me yearn
Cause the thought of you unhappy
Burns my soul
I know I caused some scars
That I want to so eagerly heal
But I'll have to live with this feeling
For my remaining years
You've meant more to me
Than I could ever imagine

The One About Better Days

Each day is a struggle
Trying to fight these feelings
Stealing minor pieces of joy
Using them as bandages to just survive another day
Nowhere to stay that is safe from these thoughts
Haunted by all the pain and trials of my past
Someone casted a spell
That has made my life a living hell
Each day is a struggle
Yet, I know there are better days
So I will just ride this wave
With all this pain
Until I can regain
All the things I lost
Along the way
Working to get better
Each and every day
Each day is a struggle

The One About Opinions

In a room full of people
Where do I stand
When they look
Who do they see
What are they thinking
How should I be
Should I play the role
Or just plain cold
They've developed the opinions
And its loud and clear
Sorry, this is my world
So you can run with fear
In a room full of people
I don't care what you see
I see a warrior
So you might want to stay clear
I am here
There's nothing I fear
In a room full of people

The One About the Keys to My Heart

Just so you know, I will always be here for you. Next to your side ready to ride because there's nothing like a you and I. I cry sometimes thinking of what had been, what should've been, and what will never be.

Each time I think of immature ways, the days I caused you to cry a river, due to my selfish ways. Written words will never fully explain the pain and sorrow I feel for those long days and lonely nights.

Somehow, as I write this it still doesn't seem like enough, and you may never read this nor will I fully be able to explain the actions of my past. All I know is that in my heart, I will always feel the pain for who I was, and what I didn't do to be a better person for you.

Unique as we were, maybe this is what was supposed to happen because I close my eyes and I picture you living the life you deserve and that whatever path you took led you to your dreams of joy and happiness because you deserve a lifetime of that.

So many things remind me of you, just the joy in your heart, the smile on your face, the energy about you that was so infectious that anyone in your presence had a present of being a part of your kind heart. So this is just a simple letter, to tell you no matter where you are, I just see the sparkle in your eyes and I will always be here for you no matter the miles.

The One About Dad's Little Girl

Those words never really felt like a crime
Until they were of mine
It turned into a mentally violent crime
I may never be able to tell her any stories
She would never be dad's little girl
Because mom decided to be a savage
Taking away the possible Apple of my eye
Now my eyes are full of tears
I would have given anything to protect you
But I was stripped of that joy
She toyed with my emotions
Making me emotionless
An Angel I'll never meet
But you'll always be remembered
Dad's little girl that never would be
I would have taken care of my child

The One Where You Pushed Me Away

If I ever made a checklist
I could check each box with you
But you too busy checking what you don't like about me
Instead of giving us a chance
And seeing where we could really be
I am over the roller coaster ride
And just want a rider for life
If you dissect us
You'll just pick us apart until there's nothing left
So if that's what you want then you're doing it right
Just know right now, I am here
And each piece you pick away
Pushes me away
So I want to stay
I want to be with you every day
But, hey it takes two
To do this
Too little time to waste on you looking for wrongs
When everything feels right
Just know if you're not careful
This love could be over tonight
If it does, it wasn't because I didn't fight

The One Where You're Meant for Me

I was so right, and I wish I was wrong
I wish I had the perfect song to explain how I feel
Just like that, our love came to an end
But I am full of hope
What we had was dope
I don't regret how things went
It just wasn't time
Even though it was Heaven sent
So I will keep my eyes on all my lucky stars
And wait for them to align
Cause in my heart
In another time
One day you'll be mine
So I've stored our memories and I hold them dear
The day you say "I do" will be the day
I shed a tear
It will be one of joy
Cause we were meant to be
Just wait until I see you again
That's when you'll know
I just hope then you can see
What I've always known
You were meant for me

The One About Dead Love

The dead speaks no evil
And, our love is dead
Yet, I would never speak any evil of you
The evil you brought with you
And the dark clouds you think you left behind
I never paid them any mind
Because they were never mine
They were all yours
So as my days got brighter
And my smile a little bigger
I figured out my worth
And knew you weren't worth my time
So the dead speaks no evil
Since you're dead to me
You have no reason to speak to me
So Ms. Evil
You should know
Your dark clouds
Don't live here anymore

The One About Breonna Taylor

Breonna Taylor
Yes, I want to say your name
Because they playing us like a game
Using us as pawns to push their agenda
As if over 400 years of oppression wasn't enough
We can't even rest in our own homes
Without getting blown away
By the ones who have an oath
To serve and protect
But they seem to serve themselves
Lie in the process
Without processing our pain
And neglect us
Because of the color of skin
When will this end?
Breonna Taylor
Let's say her name
Until she's served justice

The One About America

Black and blue
I don't know what to do
When we being battered and bruised
By ones with a badge
Kneeling on our necks
Until there's no life left
Where's our America
Because this can't be it
They spit on any advancements we make
Changing the rules
Soon as they see us progress
They are too ashamed
To admit they don't want us to rise
You can look in their eyes
And tell they want to victimize our heritage
Break our spirits
And kneel on our necks
Until we have no life left

The One About Rage

Officer
Please put away your gun
I am just hanging with friends
Trying to have some innocent fun
I spoke to my mom today
Told her I love her
And I don't want someone to give her that call
That I've fallen victim of your rage
Or a misunderstanding
That could be resolved
If you just put away your gun
Have a conversation with me
And understand I am just here with friends
Just having some innocent fun
So please don't shoot
Just please put away your gun
So I can run home
And hug my mother
And tell her I love her
And I made it home safe
While out having some innocent fun

The One About Enemies

Why am I the enemy
When all I want is a chance
To live this American dream
It seems that no matter which way I move
They want to rig the game
Make it more rigid
And socially unjust
As if we must continue to conform
To what they see as norm
And they refuse to reform a system
That's built to hold us down
They only want us around
For their own self game
They should be ashamed
Of the last 400 years
All the lies, betrayal, and injustice
So as we unite and build a new way
They want to find some way
To keep it
Like the "Good ole day"
Why am I the enemy?

The One About Chances

Just give me a chance
To address the matter
My hands are up
Please tell me that it matters
Officer, I want no harm
I will listen and obey
Just know I'll stay right here
Because losing my life I fear
I hope your body cam is on
Because I am afraid to record
Since you may mistake it for a gun
And take my life
And I know you're not all alike
But how do I know who from who
When your gun and your badge protects you
I want peace
And I want you to serve
But please don't have the nerve to stick your gun
At my face
And enforce your way
I will comply
I will not tell a lie
Cause I don't want to die
Just have your body cam on
In case I don't get a chance to say goodbye
The footage will prove
You were telling a lie
And all I wanted to do was not to die

The One About Self Love

Loving me
I had to take this journey
Which I truly can't explain
But what I learned
Is that I had to love me
Before I could find you
You were always there
Just a silhouette of the woman
Meant for me
I could see all of you in me
I just couldn't see you with me
Because you were just a silhouette
Loving me was my greatest challenge
Yet, here I am
Whole, knowing fully who I am
And what I want to be
Where I want to go
And who I want to go with
Loving me
Was the key
Just wait; you will see

The One About Loving You

Loving you
Loving you was harder than I thought
Because I thought about it too much
It was an easy thing
I just made it harder than it needed it to be
Now, I see where I went wrong
And what I need to do right
I have an "us" goal, and its full in sight
You were right all along
I needed time with me
To see who I was for me
Before I could be anything to you
Now I've learned and I know just what to do
Loving you was simple
I just made it harder than it needed it to be
Thank you for opening my eyes
Cause loving you is all I wanted to do
I just had to see it in me
While loving you

The One About Faith in Me

Dear future me,
I hope you're listening
And you hear me well
Life has been Heaven
Life has been Hell
I've walked through fire
Been burned and scorned
Been reborn by the Hands of God
Who's given me new strength
And a new will
As I sought my way
There were days
I just wanted to quit
And just give up on it all
But, a voice in my heart called
And said "This is your calling"
Just trust in me
One day you will see
Just have faith in me

The One About Blood, Sweat, and Tears

Blood, Sweat, and Tears
Masked my fears
Yet, drove me to become this being
That wanted to see
More than what was on the table
Wanted a better hand
Wanted to be a better man
Yet, every card he was dealt
Seemed to be a bust
Drove me to the edge
But I wouldn't jump
I had to keep pushing
Because I had a vision and dream
It seemed like an endless journey
With roadblocks, trials and tribulations
But those blood, sweat, and tears
Help me overcome my fears
And the fire in me
Can't be touched
I am full of life
And will conquer
Anything I touch

The One About My Life Story

Eye of the Beholder
Because, I am not ashamed
Of being different
Not fitting in
Not following the flock
Locking myself within myself
So I can sort out my thoughts
I get caught up in the moment
Even lost in time
My mind wanders
Passion hot like summer
Eye of the Beholder
Cause I am an open book
Not shook by the ones who prey on my very being
Trying to see me fail, trying to jail the person I am
I just pray for them
Eye of the Beholder, because my journey of blood, sweat, and tears
Is written in a book
A life story took right from my heart and into your soul
Eye of the Beholder

www.ingramcontent.com/pod-product-compliance
Lightning Source LLC
Chambersburg PA
CBHW031520040426
42445CB00009B/319